The CoParent's Communication Pocket Guide for:

Productive CoParenting Responses

KEVIN L SCOTT

A special thank you to my wife, Maria for bringing me the idea behind this pocket guide. And to Chelsea and Cindy for providing clarity to my words as I put them to paper. Your help was greatly appreciated!

Copyright © 2022 Kevin L Scott
All Rights Reserved.
No portion of this book may be reproduced in any form without permission from the author or publisher, except as permitted by U.S. copyright law.
ISBN: 9798218012342

CONTENTS

About The Author

How to Use this Pocket Guide

Method 1 – A Response Isn't Always Necessary

Method 2 – Be as Brief as Possible

Method 3 – Express and Enforce Your Boundaries

Method 4 – Give a Compliment

Method 5 – Shift the Focus to Your Children

Method 6 – Keep It Short and Simple (KISS)

Method 7 – Breathe Deeply and Relax Your Mind

Method 8 – Learn to Compromise

Method 9 – Actively Listen

Good CoParenting Communication Practices

Which Method May Apply To Your Situation

Closing Notes

ABOUT THE AUTHOR

My name is Kevin Scott, and I am the Founder and CEO of Build Your Wings Consulting, LLC and author of ***The 32K Format: The CoParent's Transformation Guide to Becoming a Better Person and a Better Parent***. I have a passion for adding value to coparents by helping them transform into better communicators.

For over 20 years of my life, I have been a coparent and what I have learned from my experiences as well as my research, studies and the conversations I've had with other coparents is that there was a need for a program that could help coparents resolve their communication issues. One common thing that I have identified is that the communication issues between the two parents can make life hard on the parents as well as their children and as a result, this makes it difficult for them to resolve even the simplest of issues. This is why I use my life experiences and training to help coparents work to improve their communication skills.

HOW TO USE THIS POCKET GUIDE

Did you just get an unsettling message from your coparent and now you're wondering how you're going to respond? Well now, you have an opportunity to practice some strategies that can help to guide you through some of these trying times.

This pocket guide is designed to help you work through different scenarios you may encounter when you need to reply to them. Here's the thing. You can choose to use one of the methods or combine any that you think best fits your situation, or better yet, you can modify what is written. The choice is yours.

The information is intended to help you become aware of how to manage and be more successful in your role as a coparent.

As you use this pocket guide, you will receive various ways in which you can improve your situation if it applies to you. Therefore, before you proceed, I ask that you make a commitment (for yourself and your children) to use this information with the understanding that your coparent may not have the same level of commitment as you.

Every coparenting relationship is unique, and the advice and information provided addresses general techniques that you can use so that you can calmly respond to them. Just know that these techniques are not suitable for situations where the health and safety of you or your children are put into question. In those situations, seek the proper authorities, legal assistance or a therapist, if needed.

Method 1 – A Response Isn't Always Necessary

Contrary to what some may think, you can choose what messages you will or won't give attention to from your coparent. Doing this will help to protect your sanity and give you a sense of relief. If you are aware that the communication from your coparent is argumentative and there is nothing in their message that is for the purpose of information sharing or making a decision regarding the children, then it's usually best to not respond at all.

Following this method doesn't mean that you will completely ignore any communication from your coparent. It just means that you will choose when or if you will give any attention to the message.

Some of the best ways to practice this method can be to:

- Use the "Do not disturb" option on your text messages (if available) so that you

are not alerted every time you get a message from your coparent
- Place a filter on any emails you receive from your coparent so you can prevent them from popping up as a notification on your screen
- Sleep on it by waiting until the next day to respond

When you reduce the number of ways that you can be alerted every time a message comes in from your coparent, the following things can happen:

- It releases a feeling of anxiety that you would get when you see their name pop up on your screen
- You won't feel that you are at your coparent's beck and call

NOTE – This method may not apply when you have pressing issues that are time sensitive.

Method 2 – Be as Brief as Possible

This method involves giving short replies to keep the conversation brief. If you need to discuss an important matter or have a verbal discussion regarding your children, be brief. Being brief means reducing how much you'll say to your coparent and how often you'll communicate with them. When you send a text that is just one or a few words, you can focus on other things that matter to you and go on with the rest of your day.

Here are a few ways you can be brief:

- If your coparent sends you a message and you just don't feel like going into detail or giving an elaborate answer, then think about the shortest response you can give that will satisfy as an answer.
- If you have to speak to them in person, then use simple "yes" or "no" answers when possible.
- Don't give too many words that your coparent could react to. Sometimes, the

> more you say, the more likely you are to trigger another response from them.
- If your coparent sends you a message to complain or vent about something that has happened (and you have no control over or interest in), choose a short, compassionate response. One frequently used response is: "I'm saddened to hear that."

Sounds easy to say right? Well, it actually can be that easy if you give it a try.

Method 3 – Express and Enforce Your Boundaries

This method can be used when your coparent takes advantage of the boundaries and rules that you have put in place. Your boundaries are there to protect you from behavior that might be harmful to you. Think of it this way. If something that your coparent does makes you uncomfortable or disrespects you, then that thing can tear down the boundaries you've set up, if you do not address them. So, if your coparent is pushing or violating your boundaries, listen to your gut because it's trying to give you a heads up that something's not right! Let your coparent know what treatment you will and won't accept in order to stand up for your needs. If you have to talk about facts and not opinions, share that, too. Express what's best for you and give them any rules you want them to follow to stay in contact with you.

Here are a few ways you can do this:

- Tell them if they need to contact you, to only text once a week or after work. "Please text me after work."
- You can also explain that you only have a few minutes for a respectful conversation.
- If your coparent tries to communicate with you when you don't have time or are not in the mood to talk, you can simply have an exit line ready such as, "I need to go but:
    o I have some time available to talk on (day?)"
    o I can talk between (time?) and (time?)"
- I'll reply if we keep the conversation about the children."

Method 4 – Give a Compliment

When you see your coparent doing something positive as it relates to the children, compliment them. Positive reinforcement is a key ingredient to positive coparenting. Problems often arise when coparents feel unappreciated by them. So, make a habit of acknowledging your coparent's efforts with a compliment. They may not even want the thanks, but these are the small things that go a long way towards building a good coparenting relationship.

Besides, what's the worse thing that could happen as a result of you giving your coparent a compliment? They'll get upset that you're being what... too nice?

Also, it's important to make sure that you are not giving your coparent compliments when you want something from them, or your gratitude could be perceived as a form of manipulation.

Method 5 – Shift The Focus to Your Children

If your coparent starts discussing things that are about what's going on in your life or theirs and you don't want to or feel the need to discuss it, then simply turn the conversation back to what you should only be discussing – your children. You can do this by not acknowledging their curiosity or concern and ask if there's anything that they need you to pass on to the children and then give a reason why you have to end the discussion.

Here are some examples:
- "Hello (coparent's name), Thanks for reaching out. I'm in a meeting right now but if you need to discuss something about the children, we can set up some time for some time between 5 – 5:30pm. Be well"
- "Hello (coparent's name), Everything is well, and the children are doing fine. Thanks for asking. I'll have to text you later because I don't have a lot of time right now."

- "Hi (coparent's name), you can give the children a call if you have time. I'm sure they would like to hear from you. I'm on a short suspense and need to focus. Take care."

I know this method might sound harsh but if you want to ensure that your conversations don't drift into areas that you don't want them to, sometimes you need to stop them before they can get started.

Method 6 – Keep It Short and Simple (KISS)

Your communications with your coparent must be clear so that they don't misunderstand the matter at hand. The KISS Method requires that you do not write more than a few sentences on a single topic for each message.

When sending a message to them, be respectful in your opening and closing, such as:

> "Hello (coparent's name), I am just confirming that I will be picking up (child's name) from their practice this afternoon.
>
> Thanks,
> (Your name)"

If there is a pressing deadline on a matter that requires confirmation by your coparent, be sure to address the issue as early as possible and follow up with simple messages that mention the deadline date.

If your coparent does not respond, then you have a message trail of the non-response. Also, if the issue is important, and they have a history of not responding, then end your email with something such as:

> "If I don't hear back from you by (date/day/time), then I will take that as acknowledgment that you agree to me picking up (child's name) from their practice."

Method 7 – Breathe Deeply and Relax Your Mind

After you read or hear a message from your coparent, use relaxation strategies to help you stay calm if those messages make you tense up. So, take care of yourself with some grounding exercises, such as the following:

- Set down your phone and focus on your body's reactions.
- If your muscles are clenching up, roll your shoulders and massage your jaw.
- Take ten or more deep breaths as this will help to regulate and keep you at a normal resting heart rate.
- Close your eyes and focus on relaxing every muscle group.
- Visualize an image that makes you hopeful or feel good.

When you stop and ground yourself, most feelings of anger can fade. Once you've taken that moment away from the message, you will be able to respond to the message with a clear mind.

Method 8 – Learn To Compromise

It happens from time to time that you have an issue with your coparent. But if you resort to retaliation, versus trying to work out whatever conflict or situation you may be in, you will often get stuck in a never-ending cycle of going back and forth with them.

One of the hardest yet easiest thing that you can do is to "agree to disagree" with your coparent so that you can at least make some sort of progress for your children's sake as opposed to not accomplishing anything at all.

Sometimes you and your coparent are not going to see eye to eye on certain issues related to your children. In these instances, it's important that the two of you try to work out a solution that you both can live with.

Understand that they may never see it your way. However, you can compromise and find the middle ground on most issues. The key is to minimize major issues and set boundaries so that those issues can be resolved.

Method 9 – Actively Listen

An important part of coparenting communication is listening, hearing, and feeling understood. To do this, consider the following:

- Make an honest effort to hear what message your coparent is trying to relay. If you don't, how will you be able to give them a good response to whatever it is that they are talking about?
- If you are thinking of an answer or a comeback while your coparent is talking then you are not truly listening. Take the time and listen with intent because you might hear something that you need to know.
- Listen to your coparent so that you can understand what they are trying to say before you make your mind up whether you are right or if they are wrong.

You and your coparent have to do what you can to actually listen to one another. If not for yourselves, you have to do it for the well-being of your children.

Good CoParenting Communication Practices

Here are some other communication practices you can use to help with your responses to your coparent:

- Be clear, concise, and respectful.
- Don't criticize, blame, accuse, or threaten.
- Be cooperative.
- Before you communicate, think of how your words will come across. Will you sound unreasonable or over-demanding?
- Keep texting brief.
- Set up boundaries with your co-parent on how many emails or texts are appropriate in a day.
- Let go of the past - You won't be able to successfully coparent if you have nothing but contempt for your coparent.
- Vent your frustrations with friends, family, or a therapist, but never vent to your coparent.
- Take turns speaking.

- Don't interrupt.
- If you are responding to your coparent, repeat in your own words what they said, and ask if you understood it correctly. If not, ask your coparent to rephrase it.
- Communicate directly because when you go through someone else like a stepparent, grandparent, or significant other, you run the risk of things getting miscommunicated.

Which Method May Apply To Your Situation

Which Method May Apply To Your Situation

Things your coparent may do:	Method 1: A Response Isn't Always Necessary	Method 2: Be as Brief as Possible	Method 3: Express and Enforce Your Boundaries	Method 4: Give a Compliment	Method 5: Shift the Focus to Your Children	Method 6: Keep It Short and Simple (KISS)	Method 7: Breathe Deeply and Relax Your Mind	Method 8: Learn to Compromise	Method 9: Actively Listen
They struggle to stick to agreements	●		●						●
They refuse to be flexible	●	●	●					●	●
They'll put the kids in the middle of disagreements between the two of you	●	●	●		●	●	●		●
They'll use manipulation when they want something	●	●	●		●	●	●		
They may try to spoil good things you experience with criticism	●		●		●		●		
They lack empathy	●	●	●			●	●		●
They call or send a message and expect you to answer immediately	●	●	●			●	●		
They say things to you or about you that are condescending	●		●		●	●	●		●
They criticize you in front of the children	●		●				●		
They use other people to deliver messages to you	●						●		●
They constantly need the discussion to be about them	●	●			●	●	●		●

Which Method May Apply To Your Situation

Things your coparent may do:	Method 1 A Response Isn't Always Necessary	Method 2 Be as Brief as Possible	Method 3 Express and Enforce Your Boundaries	Method 4 Give a Compliment	Method 5 Shift the Focus to Your Children	Method 6 Keep It Short and Simple (KISS)	Method 7 Breathe Deeply and Relax Your Mind	Method 8 Learn to Compromise	Method 9 Actively Listen
They blame you for problems that they may be having	●		●		●		●		
They contact you at times that are inappropriate	●		●				●		
They tend to want to discuss too many topics all at one time			●			●	●		●
They keep doing things that they know will get a rise out of you	●						●		
They feel strongly that what you are doing for the children is wrong	●		●			●	●		●
Their conversations or messages seem to drag on and on with no end in sight		●	●			●			
They feel that they are doing more than their fair share and want you to understand				●					●
They try to tell you how the children should be disciplined			●					●	●
They have little respect for your feelings, your privacy, or your things.	●		●				●		

Closing Notes

You and your coparent need to continuously and intentionally work on communicating with one another so that you can do what's best for your children. It might not be pretty at times but if you can work towards having positive and productive communication with your coparent, it will increase the likelihood that the two of you can respond to each other in a respectful manner.

Thank you for reading ***The CoParent's Communication Pocket Guide for Productive CoParenting Responses***. I hope that these methods will help with mitigating the communication issues you have now as well as those that you may encounter in the future.

www.ingramcontent.com/pod-product-compliance
Lightning Source LLC
LaVergne TN
LVHW061627070526
838199LV00070B/6612